Murphy's Law

Book ~~four~~ three

wrong reasons why things go more!

Arthur Bloch

PRICE/STERN/SLOAN
Publishers, Inc., Los Angeles
1982

Illustrated by Ed Powers

Copyright© 1982 by Arthur Bloch
Illustrations Copyright© 1982 by Price/Stern/Sloan Publishers, Inc.
Published by Price/Stern/Sloan Publishers, Inc.
410 North La Cienega Boulevard, Los Angeles, California 90048

Library of Congress Catalog Card Number: 82-61434
ISBN: 0-8431-0618-2
PSS!® is a registered trademark of Price/Stern/Sloan Publishers, Inc.

ACKNOWLEDGEMENTS AND PERMISSIONS:

Grateful acknowledgement is made to the following for permission to reprint their material.

Byrne's Law of Concreting: "Western Construction," May, 1978.

"Golomb's Don'ts of Mathematical Modeling": reprinted from "Astronautics and Aeronautics," January 1968 by permission of the American Institute of Astronautics and Aeronautics.

Finnigan's Law: "Organic Gardening," June 1978.

Fox on Bureaucracy, Decisiveness . . . etc., Disraeli's Dictum, Wilkie's Law, Things That Can be Counted on in a Crisis: from *Trapped in the Organization,* Joe Fox, Price/Stern/Sloan Publishers, Inc., Los Angeles, CA, 1980.

The Lippman Lemma: "The Worm Runner's Digest," 1979, Vol. 21, No. 1.

Lowe's Law: Frances Lowe, "Lubbock Avalanche-Journal," January 28,1979.

Macbeth's Comment on Evolution: "Towards," 17417 Vintage St., Northridge, CA, 91325, Vol. 2, No. 2.

Olivier's Law, Seeger's Law: Herb Caen's column, *San Francisco Chronicle,* Nov. 29, 1981.

Roche's Fifth Law: John P. Roche, "Albany Times-Union," July 14, 1978.

Schrank's First Law: Robert Schrank, *Ten Thousand Working Days,* MIT Press, Cambridge, Mass., 1978.

CONTENTS

INTRODUCTION

With this third volume of Murphy's Law we begin to sense the limitlessness of man's potential, especially his potential for conjuring up new Laws to explain our everyday existence.

For just as the finite contains the seed of the infinite, so does the vantage of Murphy's Law afford as good a view as any of man's place in the cosmos.

To illustrate, beginning with the finite, a major supermarket chain was accused recently of overcharging its customers; the automatic check-out machines, which read and decipher those mysterious black lines on packages, were charging inflated prices on everything from soup to nuts.

A couple of days later the Parent Company, which shall remain nameless, responded to the charge. It was all due, they said, to "human error."

We are reminded at once of the Fifth Law of Unreliability: "To err is human, but to really foul things up requires a computer." Surely, the last thing The Company wanted us to consider was "computer error," and so it seems reasonble that blame for the screw-up should be placed squarely on the only part of the machine with shoulders. Jacob's Law reminds us, "To err is human, but to blame it on someone else is even more human."

But what was The Company telling us that we didn't already know? Whether a failure is due to hardware, software or tupperware, ultimate responsibility must always rest with people, both because we built the stuff in the first place and because we are the only ones with a stake in how things turn out.

"Human error" is redundant. Of all creatures, we are the only ones capable of error — which sets us apart from animals, computers and everything else. You don't blame bad weather on "cloud error;" or a crop shortage on "plant error." Man, beside being the first life form capable of knowing himself, is also the only one capable of kicking himself.

Yet this view of people, which is so essential to Murphy's Law and to cosmology, is completely missing from the accepted, scientific world-view, in which "man" does not even constitute a special case. Thank goodness there is one commentator, at least, for whom human error is a clue that man is a very, very special case — Mae West, who said, "To err is human, but it feels divine."

ADVANCED MURPHOLOGY

MURPHY'S LAW:

If anything can go wrong, it will.

O'TOOLE'S COMMENTARY (from *Murphy's Law I*):

Murphy was an optimist.

GOLDBERG'S COMMENTARY:

O'Toole was an optimist.

NAGLER'S COMMENT ON THE ORIGIN OF MURPHY'S LAW:

Murphy's Law was not propounded by Murphy, but by another man of the same name.

KOHN'S COROLLARY TO MURPHY'S LAW:

Two wrongs are only the beginning.

McDONALD'S COROLLARY TO MURPHY'S LAW:

In any given set of circumstances, the proper course of action is determined by subsequent events.

MURPHY'S LAW OF GOVERNMENT:

If anything can go wrong, it will do so in triplicate.

MAAHS' LAW:

Things go right so they can go wrong.

ADDENDUM TO MURPHY'S LAW:

In precise mathematical terms, $1 + 1 = 2$, where "=" is a symbol meaning "seldom if ever."

MURPHY'S UNCERTAINTY PRINCIPLE:

You can know something has gone wrong only when you make an odd number of mistakes.

TUSSMAN'S LAW:

Nothing is as inevitable as a mistake whose time has come.

GUALTIERI'S LAW OF INERTIA:

Where there's a will, there's a won't.

FAHNESTOCK'S RULE FOR FAILURE:

If at first you don't succeed, destroy all evidence that you tried.

ZYMURGY'S LAW OF EVOLVING SYSTEMS DYNAMICS (from *Murphy's Law I*):

Once you open a can of worms, the only way to recan them is to use a larger can.

KAISER'S COMMENT ON ZYMURGY:

Never open a can of worms unless you plan to go fishing.

MURPHY'S MATHEMATICAL AXIOM:

For large values of one, one approaches two, for small values of two.

DUDE'S LAW DUALITY:

Of two possible events, only the undesired one will occur.

HANE'S LAW:

There is no limit to how bad things can get.

PERRUSSEL'S LAW:

There is no job so simple that it cannot be done wrong.

MAE WEST'S OBSERVATION:

To err is human, but it feels divine.

THINE'S LAW:

Nature abhors people.

BORKOWSKI'S LAW:

You can't guard against the arbitrary.

LACKLAND'S LAWS:

1. Never be first.
2. Never be last.
3. Never volunteer for anything.

THE PAROUZZI PRINCIPLE:

Given a bad start, trouble will increase at an exponential rate.

THE CHI FACTOR:

Quantity $= \dfrac{1}{\text{Quality}}$; or, quantity is inversely proportional to quality.

KEN'S LAW:

A flying particle will seek the nearest eye.

SCHOPENHAUER'S LAW OF ENTROPY:

If you put a spoonful of wine in a barrel full of sewage, you get sewage.

If you put a spoonful of sewage in a barrel full of wine, you get sewage.

ALLEN'S LAW:

Almost anything is easier to get into than to get out of.

FROTHINGHAM'S FOURTH LAW:

Urgency varies inversely with importance.

THE ROCKEFELLER PRINCIPLE:

Never do anything you wouldn't be caught dead doing.

YOUNG'S LAW OF INANIMATE MOBILITY:

All inanimate objects can move just enough to get in your way.

PROBLEMATICS

SMITH'S LAW:

No real problem has a solution.

HOARE'S LAW OF LARGE PROBLEMS
(from *Murphy's Law I*):

Inside every large problem is a small problem struggling to get out.

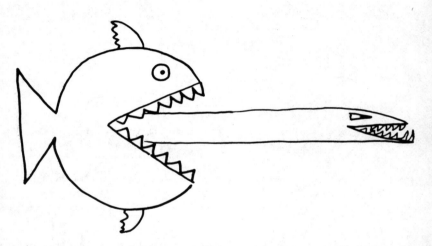

THE SCHAINKER CONVERSE TO HOARE'S LAW OF LARGE PROBLEMS:

Inside every small problem is a larger problem struggling to get out.

BIG AL'S LAW:

A good solution can be successfully applied to almost any problem.

BARUCH'S OBSERVATION:

If all you have is a hammer, everything looks like a nail.

FOX ON PROBLEMATICS:

When a problem goes away, the people working to solve it do not.

WALDROP'S PRINCIPLE:

The person not here is the one working on the problem.

BIONDI'S LAW:

If your project doesn't work, look for the part you didn't think was important.

DISRAELI'S DICTUM:

Error is often more earnest than truth.

THE ROMAN RULE:

The one who says it cannot be done should never interrupt the one who is doing it.

BLAIR'S OBSERVATION:

The best laid plans of mice and men are usually about equal.

SEAY'S LAW:

Nothing ever comes out as planned.

RUCKERT'S LAW:

There is nothing so small that it can't be blown out of proportion.

VAN HERPEN'S LAW:

The solving of a problem lies in finding the solvers.

HALL'S LAW:

The means justify the means. The approach to a problem is more important than its solution.

BAXTER'S LAW:

An error in the premise will appear in the conclusion.

McGEE'S FIRST LAW:

It's amazing how long it takes to complete something you are not working on.

HOLTEN'S HOMILE:

The only time to be positive is when you are positive you are wrong.

SEVAREID'S LAW:

The chief cause of problems is solutions.

BUREAUCRATICS
HIERARCHIOLOGY
AND
COMMITTOLOGY

THE BUREAUCRACY PRINCIPLE:

Only a bureaucracy can fight a bureaucracy.

FOX ON BUREAUCRACY:

A bureaucracy can outwait anything.

Corollary:

Never get caught between two bureaucracies.

YOUNG'S SECOND LAW:

It is the dead wood that holds up the tree.

Corollary:

Just because it is still standing, doesn't mean it is not dead.

HOFFSTEDT'S EMPLOYMENT PRINCIPLE:

Confusion creates jobs.

SOPER'S LAW:

Any bureaucracy reorganized to enhance efficiency is immediately indistinguishable from its predecessor.

GATES' LAW:

The only important information in a hierarchy is who knows what.

McKERNAN'S MAXIM:

Those who are unable to learn from past meetings are condemned to repeat them.

OWEN'S THEORY OF ORGANIZATIONAL DEVIANCE:

Every organization has an alotted number of positions to be filled by misfits.

Corollary:

Once a misfit leaves. another will be recruited.

AIGNER'S AXIOM:

> No matter how well you perform your job, a superior will seek to modify the results.

THE LIPPMAN LEMMA:

> People specialize in their area of greatest weakness.

FOX ON LEVELOLOGY:

> What will get you promoted on one level will get you killed on another.

THINGS THAT CAN BE COUNTED ON IN A CRISIS:

> **MARKETING** says yes.
>
> **FINANCE** says no.
>
> **LEGAL** has to review it.
>
> **PERSONNEL** is concerned.
>
> **PLANNING** is frantic.
>
> **ENGINEERING** is above it all.
>
> **MANUFACTURING** wants more floor space.
>
> **TOP MANAGEMENT** wants someone responsible.

COURTOIS' RULE:

> If people listened to themselves more often, they would talk less.

HUTCHINS' LAW:

You can't outtalk a man who know what he's talking about.

FAHNSTOCK'S THIRD LAW OF DEBATE:

Any issue worth debating is worth avoiding altogether.

HARTZ'S LAW OF RHETORIC:

Any argument carried far enough will end up in semantics.

MITCHELL'S LAWS OF COMMITTOLOGY:

1. Any simple problem can be made insoluble if enough conferences are held to discuss it.

2. Once the way to screw up a project is presented for consideration it will invariably be accepted as the soundest solution.

3. After the solution screws up the project, all those who initially endorsed it will say, "I wish I had voiced my reservations at the time."

KIM'S RULE OF COMMITTEES:

If an hour has been spent amending a sentence, someone will move to delete the paragraph.

THE ELEVENTH COMMANDMENT:

Thou shalt not committee.

KENNEDY'S COMMENT ON COMMITTEES:

A committee is twelve men doing the work of one.

SWEENEY'S LAW:

The length of a progress report is inversely proportional to the amount of progress.

MORRIS' LAW OF CONFERENCES:

The most interesting paper will be scheduled simultaneously with the second most interesting paper.

THIRD LAW OF COMMITTO-DYNAMICS:

Those most opposed to serving on committees are made chairmen.

STATESMANSHIP

HELGA'S RULE:

Say no, then negotiate.

BROWN'S RULES OF LEADERSHIP:

1. To succeed in politics, it is often necessary to rise above your principles.

2. The best way to succeed in politics is to find a crowd that's going somewhere and get in front of them.

THE RULE OF LAW:

If the facts are against you, argue the law.

If the law is against you, argue the facts.

If the facts and the law are against you, yell like hell.

MILES' LAW (from *Murphy's Law II*):

Where you stand depends on where you sit.

FIBLEY'S EXTENSION TO MILES' LAW:

Where you sit depends on who you know.

FOX ON POWER:

Arrogance is too often the companion of excellence.

WALTON'S LAW OF POLITICS:

A fool and his money are soon elected.

THE FIFTH RULE OF POLITICS:

When a politician gets an idea, he usually gets it wrong.

WILKIE'S LAW:

A good slogan can stop analysis for fifty years.

SHERMAN'S RULE OF PRESS CONFERENCES:

The explanation of a disaster will be made by a stand-in.

ROCHE'S FIFTH LAW:

Every American crusade winds up as a racket.

MILLER'S LAW:

Exceptions prove the rule — and wreck the budget.

BUCHWALD'S LAW:

As the economy gets better, everything else gets worse.

OGDEN NASH'S LAW:

Progress may have been all right once, but it went on too long.

FINNIGAN'S LAW:

The farther away the future is, the better it looks.

SIMON'S LAW OF DESTINY:

Glory may be fleeting, but obscurity is forever.

THOMPSON'S THEOREM:

When the going gets weird, the weird turn pro.

FIRST LAW OF POLITICS:

Stay in with the outs.

LAW OF PROMOTIONAL TOURS:

Jet lag accumulates unit directionally toward maximum difficulty to perform.

ROBBINS' MINI-MAX RULE OF GOVERNMENT:

Any minimum criteria set will be the maximum value used.

LOWE'S LAW:

Success always occurs in private, and failure in full public view.

EXPERTSMANSHIP

HOROWITZ'S RULE:

Wisdom consists of knowing when to avoid perfection.

DE NEVERS' LAW OF COMPLEXITY:

The simplest subjects are the ones you don't know anything about.

CHRISTIE-DAVIES' THEORUM:

If your facts are wrong but your logic is perfect, then your conclusions are inevitably false. Therefore, by making mistakes in your logic, you have at least a random chance of coming to a correct conclusion.

McCLELLAN'S LAW OF COGNITION:

Only new categories escape the stereotyped thinking associated with old abstractions.

HARTZ'S UNCERTAINTY PRINCIPLE:

Ambiguity is invariant.

DE NEVERS' LAW OF DEBATE:

Two monologues do not make a dialogue.

EMERSON'S OBSERVATION:

In every work of genius we recognize our rejected thoughts.

HIRAM'S LAW:

If you consult enough experts you can confirm any opinion.

JORDAN'S LAW:

An informant who never produces misinformation is too deviant to be trusted.

DE NEVERS' LOST LAW:

Never speculate on that which can be known for certain.

LAS VEGAS LAW:

Never bet on a loser because you think his luck is bound to change.

VAN ROY'S SECOND LAW:

If you can distinguish between good advice and bad advice, then you don't need advice.

HOWE'S LAW (from *Murphy's Law I*):

Everyone has a scheme that will not work.

MUNDER'S COROLLARY TO HOWE'S LAW:

Everyone who does not work has a scheme that does.

FOX ON DECISIVENESS:

1. Decisiveness is not in itself a virtue.
2. To decide not to decide is a decision.
   To fail to decide is a failure.
3. An important reason for an executive's existence is to make sensible exceptions to policy.

ELY'S KEY TO SUCCESS:

Create a need, and fill it.

BRALEK'S RULE FOR SUCCESS:

Trust only those who stand to lose as much as you when things go wrong.

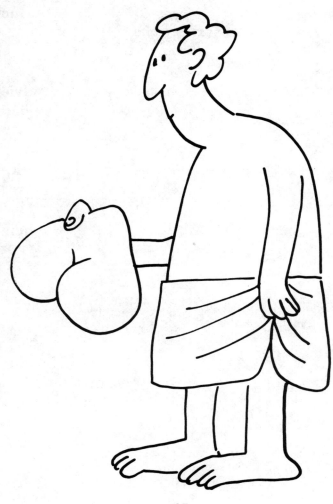

DESIGNSMANSHIP

POULSEN'S PROPHESY:

If anything is used to its full potential, it will break.

MAYNE'S LAW:

Nobody notices the big errors.

PRINCIPLE OF DESIGN INERTIA:

Any change looks terrible at first.

ENG'S PRINCIPLE:

The easier it is to do, the harder it is to change.

ROBERTSON'S LAW:

Quality assurance doesn't.

WRIGHT'S FIRST LAW OF QUALITY:

Quality is inversely proportional to the time left for completion of the project.

EDWARDS' TIME/EFFORT LAW:

Effort X Time = Constant

A. Given a large initial time to do something the initial effort will be small.

B. As time goes to zero, effort goes to infinity.

Corollary:

If it weren't for the last minute, nothing would get done.

FIRST LAW OF CORPORATE PLANNING:

Anything that can be changed will be changed until there is no time left to change anything.

BEACH'S LAW:

No two identical parts are alike.

WILLOUGHBY'S LAW:

When you try to prove to someone that a machine won't work, it will.

THE BASIC LAW OF CONSTRUCTION:

Cut it large and kick it into place.

MEISSNER'S LAW:

Any producing entity is the last to use its own product.

MACPHERSON'S THEORY OF ENTROPY:

It requires less energy to take an object out of its proper place than to put it back.

SPECIAL LAW:

The workbench is always untidier than last time.

GENERAL LAW:

The chaos in the universe always increases.

SCHRANK'S FIRST LAW:

If it doesn't work, expand it.

Corollary:

The greater the magnitude, the less notice will be taken that it does not work.

BITTON'S POSTULATE
ON STATE-OF-THE-ART ELECTRONICS:

If you understand it, it's obsolete.

MANUBAY'S LAWS FOR PROGRAMMERS:

1. If a programmer's modification of an existing program works, it's probably not what the users want.

2. Users don't know what they really want, but they know for certain what they don't want.

JOSE'S AXIOM:

Nothing is as temporary as that which is called permanent.

Corollary:

Nothing is as permanent as that which is called temporary.

WASHLESKY'S LAW:

Anything is easier to take apart than to put together.

RUDNICKI'S RULE:

That which cannot be taken apart will fall apart.

RAP'S LAW OF INANIMATE REPRODUCTION:

If you take something apart and put it back together enough times, eventually you will have two of them.

RESEARCHMANSHIP
AND
ACADEMIOLOGY

FREIVALD'S LAW:

Only a fool can reproduce another fool's work.

TENENBAUM'S LAW OF REPLICABILITY:

The most interesting results happen only once.

SOUDER'S LAW:

Repetition does not establish validity.

HANGGI'S LAW:

The more trivial your research, the more people will read it and agree.

Corollary:

The more vital your research, the less people will understand it.

HANDY GUIDE TO MODERN SCIENCE
(from *Murphy's Law II*):

1. If it's green or it wriggles, it's biology.

2. If it stinks, it's chemistry.

3. If it doesn't work, it's physics.

CERF'S EXTENSIONS TO THE HANDY GUIDE TO MODERN SCIENCE:

4. If it's incomprehensible, it's mathematics.

5. If it doesn't make sense, it's either economics or psychology.

YOUNG'S COMMENT ON SCIENTIFIC METHOD:

You can't get here from there.

MACBETH'S COMMENT ON EVOLUTION:

The best theory is not *ipso facto* a good theory.

BARR'S INERTIAL PRINCIPLE:

Asking a group of scientists to revise their theory is like asking a group of cops to revise the law.

THE SAGAN FALLACY:

To say a human being is nothing but molecules is like saying a Shakespearean play is nothing but words.

THE RELIABILITY PRINCIPLE:

The difference between the Laws of Nature and Murphy's Law is that with the Laws of Nature you can count on things screwing up the same way every time.

DARWIN'S LAW:

Nature will tell you a direct lie if she can.

BLOCH'S EXTENSION:

So will Darwinists.

FIRST LAW OF SCIENTIFIC PROGRESS:

The advance of science can be measured by the rate at which exceptions to previously held laws accumulate.

Corollaries:

1. Exceptions always outnumber rules.
2. There are always exceptions to established exceptions.
3. By the time one masters the exceptions, no one recalls the rules to which they apply.

FIRST LAW OF PARTICLE PHYSICS:

The shorter the life of the particle, the greater it costs to produce.

SECOND LAW OF PARTICLE PHYSICS:

The basic building blocks of matter do not occur in nature.

EINSTEIN'S OBSERVATION:

Inasmuch as the mathematical theorems are related to reality, they are not sure; inasmuch as they are sure, they are not related to reality.

FINMAN'S LAW OF MATHEMATICS:

Nobody wants to read anyone else's formulas.

"GOLOMB'S DON'TS OF MATHEMATICAL MODELING":

1. Don't believe the 33rd order consequences of a 1st order model.
   CATCH PHRASE: "Cum grano salis."

2. Don't extrapolate beyond the region of fit.
   CATCH PHRASE: "Don't go off the deep end."

3. Don't apply any model until you understand the simplifying assumptions on which it is based, and can test their applicability.

   CATCH PHRASE: "Use only as directed."

4. Don't believe that the model is the reality.
   CATCH PHRASE: "Don't eat the menu."

5. Don't distort reality to fit the model.
   CATCH PHRASE: "The 'Procrustes Method'."

6. Don't limit yourself to a single model: More than one may be useful for understanding different aspects of the same phenomenon.
   CATCH PHRASE: "Legalize polygamy."

7. Don't retain a discredited model.
   CATCH PHRASE: "Don't beat a dead horse."

8. Don't fall in love with your model.
   CATCH PHRASE: "Pygmalion."

9. Don't apply the terminology of Subject A to the problems of Subject B if it is to the enrichment of neither.

   CATCH PHRASE: "New names for old."

10. Don't expect that by having named a demon you have destroyed him.

    CATCH PHRASE: "Rumplestiltskin."

FELSON'S LAW:

To steal ideas from one person is plagiarism; to steal from many is research.

VALERY'S LAW:

History is the science of what never happens twice.

DARROW'S COMMENT ON HISTORY:

History repeats itself. That's one of the things wrong with history.

**PAVLU'S RULES FOR ECONOMY
IN RESEARCH:**

1. Deny the last established truth on the list.
2. Add yours.
3. Pass the list.

MR. COOPER'S LAW (from *Murphy's Law I* **):**

If you do not understand a particular word in a piece of technical writing, ignore it. The piece will make perfect sense without it.

**BOGOVICH'S COROLLARY
TO MR. COOPER'S LAW:**

If the piece makes no sense without the word, it will make no sense with the word.

**MEREDITH'S LAW FOR GRAD
SCHOOL SURVIVAL:**

Never let your major professor know that you exist.

ELLARD'S LAW:

Those who want to learn will learn.

Those who do not want to learn will lead enterprises.

Those incapable of either learning or leading will regulate scholarship and enterprise to death.

VILE'S LAW FOR EDUCATORS:

No one is listening until you make a mistake.

SEEGER'S LAW:

Anything in parentheses can be ignored.

VILE'S LAW OF GRADING PAPERS:

All papers after the top are upside down or backwards, until you right the pile. Then the process repeats.

WEINER'S LAW OF LIBRARIES:

There are no answers, only cross-references.

OFFICE-MURPHOLOGY

LAUNEGAYER'S OBSERVATION:

Asking dumb questions is easier than correcting dumb mistakes.

BOGOVICH'S LAW:

He who hesitates is probably right.

STRANO'S LAW:

When all else fails, try the boss's suggestion.

BRINTNALL'S SECOND LAW:

If you are given two contradictory orders, obey them both.

SHAPIRO'S LAW OF REWARD:

The one who does the least work will get the most credit.

JOHNSON'S LAW:

The number of minor illnesses among the employees is inversely proportional to the health of the organization.

TILLIS' ORGANIZATIONAL PRINCIPLE:

If you file it, you'll know where it is but never need it.
If you don't file it, you'll need it but never know where it is.

OWEN'S LAW FOR SECRETARIES:

As soon as you sit down to a cup of hot coffee, your boss will ask you to do something which will last until the coffee is cold.

SANDILAND'S LAW:

Free time which unexpectedly becomes available will be wasted.

DOANE'S LAWS OF PROCRASTINATION:

1. The more proficient one is at procrastination, the less proficient one need be at all else.

2. The slower one works, the fewer mistakes one makes.

SCOTT'S LAW OF BUSINESS:

Never walk down a hallway in an office building without a piece of paper in your hand.

HARBOUR'S LAW:

The deadline is one week after the original deadline.

EDDIE'S FIRST LAW OF BUSINESS:

Never conduct negotiations before 10 A.M. or after 4 P.M. Before 10 you appear too anxious, and after 4 they think you're desperate.

TABLE OF HANDY OFFICE EXCUSES:

1. That's the way we've always done it.
2. I didn't know you were in a hurry for it.
3. That's not my department.
4. No one told me to go ahead.
5. I'm waiting for an O.K.
6. How did I know this was different?
7. That's his job, not mine.
8. Wait 'til the boss comes back and ask him.
9. We don't make many mistakes.
10. I didn't think it was very important.
11. I'm so busy, I just can't get around to it.
12. I thought I told you.
13. I wasn't hired to do that.

DRUMMOND'S LAW OF PERSONNEL RECRUITING:

The ideal resume will turn up one day after the position is filled.

GLUCK'S FIRST LAW:

Whichever way you turn upon entering an elevator, the buttons will be on the opposite side.

LYNCH'S LAW:

The elevator always comes after you have put down your bag.

FOX ON YESMANSHIP:

It's worth scheming to be the bearer of good news.

Corollary:

Don't be in the building when bad news arrives.

PINTO'S LAW:

Do someone a favor and it becomes your job.

CONNOR'S SECOND LAW:

If something is confidential, it will be left in the copier machine.

LANGSAM'S ORNITHOLOGICAL AXIOM:

It's difficult to soar with eagles when you work with turkeys.

HOUSEHOLD MURPHOLOGY

PAUL'S LAW (from *Murphy's Law I*):

You can't fall off the floor.

CHAPMAN'S COMMENTARY ON PAUL'S LAW:

It takes children three years to learn Paul's Law.

RINGWALD'S LAW OF HOUSEHOLD GEOMETRY:

Any horizontal surface is soon piled up.

THE PINEAPPLE PRINCIPLE:

The best parts of anything are always impossible to remove from the worst parts.

O'TOOLE'S AXIOM:

One child is not enough, but two children are far too many.

RELATIVITY FOR CHILDREN:

Time moves slower in a fast moving vehicle.

DINER'S DILEMMA:

A clean tie attracts the soup of the day.

THIESSEN'S LAW OF GASTRONOMY:

The hardness of the butter is in direct proportion to the softness of the roll.

BELL'S THEOREM:

When a body is immersed in water, the telephone rings.

WOODSIDE'S GROCERY PRINCIPLE:

The bag that breaks is the one with the eggs.

STITZER'S VACATION PRINCIPLE:

When packing for a vacation, take half as much clothing and twice as much money.

SNIDER'S LAW:

Nothing can be done in one trip.

ESTHER'S LAW:

The fussiest person will be the one to get the chipped coffee cup, the glass with lipstick or the hair in the food.

POPE'S LAW:

Chipped dishes never break.

THE PET PRINCIPLE:

No matter which side of the door the dog or cat is on, it is the wrong side.

BOREN'S LAW FOR CATS:

When in doubt, wash.

HOROWITZ'S LAW:

Whenever you turn on the radio, you hear the last few notes of your favorite song.

GERARD'S LAW:

When there are sufficient funds in the checking account, checks take two weeks to clear. When there are insufficient funds, checks clear overnight.

LAW OF SUPERMARKETS:

The quality of the house brand varies inversely with the size of the supermarket chain.

SEYMOUR'S INVESTMENT PRINCIPLE:

Never invest in anything that eats.

LAST LAW OF PRODUCT DESIGN:

If you can't fix it, feature it.

PANTUSO'S FIRST LAW:

The book you spent $10.95 for today will come out in paperback tomorrow.

RILEY'S "MURPHY'S LAW" LAWS:

1. Stores that sell Volume One will not know of Volume Two.

2. Stores that sell Volume Two will be out of Volume One.

3. Ed Murphy has not heard of either book.

VILE'S LAW OF VALUE:

The more an item costs, the farther you have to send it for repairs.

FINMAN'S BARGAIN BASEMENT PRINCIPLE (from *Murphy's Law II*):

The one you want is never the one on sale.

BAKER'S COROLLARY TO FINMAN'S BARGAIN BASEMENT PRINCIPLE:

You never want the one you can afford.

MURRAY'S LAWS:

1. Never ask a barber if you need a haircut.

2. Never ask a salesman if his is a good price.

GLASER'S LAW:

If it says "one size fits all," it doesn't fit anyone.

GOLDENSTERN'S RULES:

1. Always hire a rich attorney.

2. Never buy from a rich salesman.

PSYCHO-MURPHOLOGY OF EVERYDAY LIFE

SIGSTAD'S LAW:

When it gets to be your turn, they change the rules.

THE POKER PRINCIPLE:

Never do card tricks for the group you play poker with.

STENDERUP'S LAW:

The sooner you fall behind, the more time you will have to catch up.

WAGNER'S LAW OF SPORTS COVERAGE:

When the camera isolates on a male athlete, he will spit, pick or scratch.

DORR'S LAW OF ATHLETICS:

In an otherwise empty locker room, any two individuals will have adjoining lockers.

LEFTY GOMEZ'S LAW:

If you don't throw it, they can't hit it.

LAW OF PRACTICE:

Plays that work in theory do not work in practice.
Plays that work in practice do not work during the game.

GRANDPA CHARNOCK'S LAW:

You never really learn to swear until you learn to drive.

VILE'S LAW OF ROADSMANSHIP:

Your own car uses more gas and oil than anyone else's.

PHILLIPS' LAW:

Four-wheel-drive just means getting stuck in more inaccessible places.

EDDS' LAW OF RADIOLOGY:

The colder the X-Ray table, the more of your body you are required to place on it.

CROSBY'S LAW:

You can tell how bad a musical is by how many times the chorus yells, "hooray."

BYRNE'S LAW OF CONCRETING:

When you pour, it rains.

FULTON'S LAW OF GRAVITY:

The effort to catch a falling, breakable object will produce more destruction than if the object had been allowed to fall in the first place.

VILE'S LAW OF ADVANCED LINESMANSHIP:

1. If you're running for a short line, it suddenly becomes a long line.

2. When you're waiting in a long line, the people behind you are shunted to a new, short line.

3. If you step out of a short line for a second, it becomes a long line.

4. If you're in a short line, the people in front let in their friends and relatives and make it a long line.

5. A short line outside a building becomes a long line inside.

6. If you stand in one place long enough, you make a line.

HOWDEN'S LAW:

You remember to mail a letter only when you're nowhere near a mailbox.

LAWS OF POSTAL DELIVERY:

1. Love letters, business contracts and money you are due always arrive three weeks late.
2. Junk mail arrives the day it was sent.

McLAUGHLIN'S LAW:

In a key position in every geneology you will find a John Smith from London.

WRIGHT'S LAW:

A doctor can bury his mistakes, but an architect can only advise his client to plant vines.

RUSH'S RULE OF GRAVITY:

When you drop change at a vending machine, the pennies will fall nearby while all other coins will roll out of sight.

REYNOLD'S LAW OF CLIMATOLOGY:

Wind velocity increases directly with the cost of the hairdo.

SOCIO-MURPHOLOGY

SARTRE'S OBSERVATION:

Hell is others.

DOOLEY'S LAW:

Trust everybody, but cut the cards.

ZAPPA'S LAW:

There are two things on earth that are universal, hydrogen and stupidity.

GRELB'S REMINDER:

Eighty percent of all people consider themselves to be above average drivers.

MUNDER'S THEOREM:

For every "10" there are 10 "1's."

DYKSTRA'S LAW:

Everybody is somebody else's weirdo.

MEYERS' LAW:

In a social situation, that which is most difficult to do is usually the right thing to do.

YOUNG'S PRINCIPLE ON EMERGENT INDIVIDUATION:

Everybody wants to peel his own banana.

COHEN'S SECOND LAW:

People are divided into two groups—the righteous and the unrighteous—and the righteous do the dividing.

RULE OF THE OPEN MIND:

People who are resistant to change cannot resist change for the worst.

WEATHERWAX'S POSTULATE:

The degree to which you overreact to information will be in inverse proportion to its accuracy.

THE IRE PRINCIPLE:

Never try to pacify someone at the height of his rage.

THIESSEN'S LAW OF ART:

The overwhelming prerequisite for the greatness of an artist is that artist's death.

KENT FAMILY LAW:

Never change your plans because of the weather.

ELY'S LAW:

Wear the right costume and the part plays itself.

FIRST RULE OF ACTING:

Whatever happens, look as if it were intended.

PYTHON'S PRINCIPLE OF TV MORALITY:

There is nothing wrong with sex on television, just as long as you don't fall off.

LIVINGSTON'S LAWS OF FAT:

1. Fat expands to fill any apparel worn.
2. A fat person walks in the middle of the hall.

Corollary:

Two fat people will walk side by side, whether they know each other or not.

LAW OF ARRIVAL:

Those who live closest arrive latest.

ZADRA'S LAW OF BIOMECHANICS:

The severity of the itch is inversely proportional to the reach.

THE THREE LEAST CREDIBLE SENTENCES IN THE ENGLISH LANGUAGE:

1. "The check is in the mail."
2. "Of course I'll respect you in the morning."
3. "I'm from the government and I'm here to help you."

VOLTAIRE'S LAW:

There is nothing more respectable than an ancient evil.

COSMO-
MURPHOLOGY

OLIVIER'S LAW:

Experience is something you don't get until just after you need it.

FIRST RULE OF PATHOLOGY:

Most well-trodden paths lead nowhere.

GABIROL'S OBSERVATION:

The wise are pleased when they discover truth, fools when they discover falsehood.

FOSTER'S LAW:

The only people who find what they are looking for in life are the fault-finders.

FIRST PRINCIPLE OF SELF-DETERMINATION:

What you resist, you become.

STEINER'S PRECEPTS:

1. Knowledge based on external evidence is unreliable.
2. Logic can never decide what is possible or impossible.

COLRIDGE'S LAW:

Extremes meet.

FEINBERG'S SECOND PRINCIPLE:

Memory serves its own master.

LAST LAW OF ROBOTICS:

The only real errors are human errors.

YOUNG'S THIRD LAW:

It is when you trip over your own shoes that you start picking up shoes.

HOFFER'S LAW:

When people are free to do as they please, they usually imitate each other.

BERRA'S FIRST LAW:

You can observe a lot just by watching.

BERRA'S SECOND LAW:

Anyone who is popular is bound to be disliked.

PERLSWEIG'S SECOND LAW:

Whatever goes around, comes around.

MEADOW'S MAXIM:

You can't push on a rope.

OPPENHEIMER'S LAW:

There is no such thing as instant experience.

DISIMONI'S RULE OF COGNITION:

Believing is seeing.

THE SIDDHARTHA PRINCIPLE:

You cannot cross a river in two strides.

KIERKEGAARD'S OBSERVATION:

Life can only be understood backwards, but it must be lived forward.

LORD BALFOUR'S CONTENTION:

Nothing matters very much, and very few things matter at all.

INDEX

Use this index as a guide to finding your favorite laws. Laws are listed by general subject matter. The designations *I, II,* and *III* refer to the books MURPHY'S LAW AND OTHER REASONS WHY THINGS GO WRONG!, MURPHY'S LAW/BOOK TWO and MURPHY'S LAW/BOOK THREE. The number following the Roman Numeral refers to the page on which a law dealing with the subject is found.

INDEX

This book is published by

PRICE/STERN/SLOAN
Publishers, Inc., Los Angeles

whose other splendid titles include such literary classics as:

**MURPHY'S LAW AND OTHER
REASONS WHY THINGS GO WRONG! ($2.95)
MURPHY'S LAW/BOOK TWO ($2.95)
ART AFTERPIECES ($3.95)
LEGAL GUIDE TO MOTHER GOOSE ($2.95)
HOW TO BE A JEWISH MOTHER ($2.50)
HOW TO BE AN ITALIAN ($2.95)
INCREDIBLE INSURANCE CLAIMS ($2.95)**

and many, many more

They are available wherever books are sold, or may
be ordered directly from the publisher by sending check
or money order for total amount plus $1.00 for handling
and mailing. For a complete list of titles send a *stamped,
self-addressed envelope* to:

PRICE/STERN/SLOAN *Publishers, Inc.*
410 North La Cienega Boulevard, Los Angeles, California 90048